Sailing for Glory

The Story of
Angus Walters

Sailing for Glory

The Story of Angus Walters

by

Teri-Lynn Janveau
and Allister Thompson

Illustrations by Samantha Thompson

Napoleon Publishing

Napoleon Publishing
Toronto Ontario Canada

Le Conseil des Arts | The Canada Council
du Canada | for the Arts
Depuis 1957 | since 1957

Napoleon Publishing acknowledges
the support of the Canada Council
for our publishing program.

Printed in Canada

10 09 08 07 06   5 4 3 2 1

Library and Archives Canada Cataloguing in Publication

Janveau, Teri-Lynn, 1974-
    Sailing for glory : the story of Captain Angus Walters and the
Bluenose / Teri-Lynn Janveau, Allister Thompson.

Includes bibliographical references and index.
ISBN 1-894917-09-X

    1. Walters, Angus, 1882-1968--Juvenile literature.
2. Ship captains--Nova Scotia--Biography--Juvenile literature. 3. Bluenose
(Ship)--History--Juvenile literature. I. Thompson, Allister, 1974- II. Title.
VK140.W25J35 2006   j387.5092   C2006-905613-7

A Canadian Legend

Whenever you look at a Canadian dime, you see an exciting piece of history. A sailing ship called a schooner flies across the water with its sails full of strong ocean winds. In 1937, the government of Canada commemorated the deeds of this famous ship and its legendary captain on this coin, and the image is still in use today.

From 1921 to 1938, Captain Angus Walters of Lunenburg, Nova Scotia, guided *Bluenose* to victory in five international sailing races, going undefeated for an incredible seventeen years. The story of Angus Walters and his ship is in many ways the story of every fisherman on the shores of Atlantic Canada, where many men made their living on the ocean, fishing on the shallow banks in rough and fair weather. It was a hard and dangerous life, but one of pride and dignity as well.

A sense of pride was what the achievements of Angus Walters and *Bluenose* gave to their province, and to all Canadians, as they brought glory to their country.

Lunenburg

BLUENOSE

Legend has it that the name was used for Maritimers because of blue-coloured potatoes which were shipped to the United States in the eighteenth century. Another suggested origin is that it described the colour of Nova Scotians' noses in winter!

Lunenburg was, and still is, one of the largest and most beautiful communities on Nova Scotia's South Shore. It is located about ninety-two kilometres south of Halifax, the capital and largest city of Nova Scotia. The town was settled by Germans, Swiss and a few French people. It was named after the Duke of Braunschweig-Lüneburg, who became king of England in 1727. The royal family of England has German origins. Settlers were promised free land if they would come over to the New World.

All kinds of people could be found passing through the town, from places like France, Scandinavia and Newfoundland, which would not become part of Canada until 1949.

The town was prosperous, and from the beginning, much of its industry was focussed on fishing and shipbuilding. Lunenburg was probably the most prominent fishing community in the province, and it spawned many generations of hard-working sailors and captains.

The main street of Lunenburg around the turn of the twentieth century

Different Roles

LONG JOURNEYS

During the fishing season, schooners would go to the fishing banks, staying up to eight weeks at one time, or until their holds were full of cleaned and salted cod.

RECRUITMENT

Captains looking for crews went to the bars ("grog shops") to recruit sailors. They might try to lure sailors to sign up with them by getting them drunk and impairing their judgment. In the same way, in England, "press gangs" were sent out to capture unlucky men and force them to join the navy.

There were many jobs that had to be performed to make the fishing industry run properly. Shipwrights worked on building the fishing boats, blacksmiths made the hooks, gaffs (a free-swinging spar, or pole, attached to the top of the sail), spikes and iron fittings. Coopers made barrels for salt, water and the ships' other supplies. Sail makers made the sails, and rope makers wove ropes for the ships.

The women of the community prepared foods for the long voyages, which had to be specially dried to last. They also knitted sweaters and mittens for protection against the powerful, freezing North Atlantic winds. They tended vegetable gardens and ran inns and boarding houses for fishermen visiting from other places.

Fishing was the focus of life in Lunenburg. From April to September every year, the boats went out to provide a livelihood for the community.

The Lunenburg fishing fleet at the docks

A Family of Fishermen

WREATHS

Every spring, when the ships went out to sea for the first time, they carried wreaths, one for each sailor from the town who had been lost at sea the year before.

Angus Walters was born in Lunenburg on June 9, 1881, to Elias and Adelaide Walters. He was christened James Angus Walters, but later in life went by Angus J. Walters. Families were generally large in those days, and the Walters family was no exception. Angus had eleven brothers and sisters.

His father was the captain of his own fishing schooner, the *Nyanza.* Ship's captains were important people in Nova Scotia's fishing communities. Fishing on the banks was a rough and dangerous occupation, and ships would go on trips of two or three months, fishing until their holds were full. Shipwrecks on the stormy Atlantic were common, and many fishermen would never return home again.

Still, young Angus listened eagerly to his father's stories of adventure and danger on the ocean and was filled with excitement at the thought of going to sea himself one day, and maybe even becoming the captain of his own ship.

A Large Family

Families were generally much larger in those days, and children started work early to bring in money for the family. There were twelve children in Elias and Adelaide Walters' family, seven girls and five boys.

Three of the sons became sea captains, John (Sonny), Angus and Perry. Angus's sister Ella Mary, the eldest, was married to a worker at the Smith and Rhuland shipyard where *Bluenose* was built. Louisa Florence married Capt. Ammon Zinck of Lunenburg.

John "Sonny" was the eldest boy. He later lived next door to Angus and was captaining *Bluenose* in the summer of 1930 when it ran aground. Lilla Harriet moved to the United States. Carrie Belle moved to Calgary in Canada's new West. Jennie Beulah later lived two doors from Angus in the family's old house. Perry Edward was a captain who later moved to Toronto. Aubrey Lowell moved to Massachusetts, home of Angus's later American rivals. Muriel Blanche eventually moved to New York. Two other children died when they were very young.

Large families were much more common in the nineteenth century

LOTS OF SIBLINGS

Ella, born 1875
Louisa, 1876
John, 1876
Lilla, 1879
Angus, 1881
Carrie, 1882
Perry, 1886
Jennie, 1889
Aubrey, 1891
Muriel, 1896

COD

The main staple fish was Atlantic cod. Codfish vary in size and can weigh up to forty pounds (about eighteen kilograms). Eleven million pounds (almost five million kilograms) of cod were taken from the banks each year during the first twenty-five years of the century. Today the cod supply is endangered due to overfishing.

The Banks

The fishing banks were the lifeblood of Atlantic Canada's fishing industry. The banks are a submerged plateau of 194,250 square kilometres (75,000 square miles) off the coasts of Nova Scotia and Newfoundland, stretching down to the coast of New England in the United States.

Different parts of the banks area have their own names, like Banquereau, Sable Island Bank, St. Pierre Bank, Artimon, Canso, Green, Emerald, Misaine and the 93,240 square kilometre (36,000 square miles) Grand Bank, which is located to the southeast of the island of Newfoundland. These shallow regions, which are part of the continental shelf, were the best place to catch large quantities of Atlantic cod, halibut and flounder.

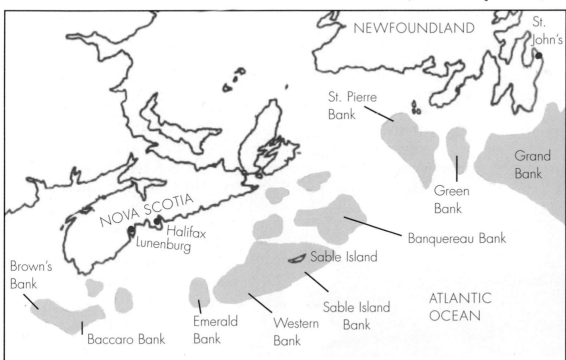

A Sailor's Life

BIG BUSINESS

During the first part of the twentieth century, Nova Scotia ruled the North Atlantic fishery. At one point, 155 vessels, employing over 2,500 men, sailed out of Lunenburg, and there were many other fishing villages along the South Shore.

SUPERSTITIONS

Sailors could be superstitious people. Some things that were considered back luck:
—Never launch a ship on Friday
—Red mittens are bad luck
—Good fortune would come to a ship that tied up at the western side of a wharf
—Never throw eggshells overboard
—Never say "pig" on board
—Sailors can sing, but should never whistle

The traditional way of life of a fisherman is now long gone and only remembered by a few elderly people and in history books.

Fishermen themselves passed on a tradition in story and song that is part of the culture of the Atlantic provinces to this day.

In those days, men started work younger than today, while still young teenagers or even earlier. There were many positions on the ships, such as cook, dorymen who went out in the dories (small boats) to set the lines, throaters who cut the fish open when they were brought on board and headers who removed the entrails and cast them overboard, and broke the head off on the end of the "dressing" table. There were also splitters who took a broad, curved knife and removed the backbone, splitting the fish open for salting, and a flunkey, an all-purpose labourer who helped the cook, the fish dressers and the dorymen. Of course, there were also the

SHARKS
Fisherman were not fond of sharks. Sharks attracted by the fish hung around the dories and could be dangerous.

captain and the first mate, the second in command, who often worked as a doryman as well.

Life on board was hard work, and it was also tedious being confined to a small ship for months. By day, sailors sang sea shanties (work songs) in rhythm with their work. At night, they would tell stories until the lamps were extinguished. There was little variety in their diet—they ate a good deal of haddock or cod. Other energy-rich foods the sailors would eat were baked beans, salt beef and salt pork, potatoes, turnips and sauerkraut. The cook made bread, cakes, cookies and pies. Tea and coffee were available all the time. There were also occasional treats like fish hearts and onions, and fried cod heads. Alcohol was often part of the daily ration. The drink was usually grog, which is rum diluted with water.

There were many medical problems associated with the hard life. Sailors had their own peculiar problems, like salt water boils. The only treatment was a linseed (another name for flax seed) poultice (a dressing). Often teeth had to be pulled out and broken bones treated with splints by fellow sailors, with only alcohol as an anesthetic.

Schooners

Schooners were the lifeblood of North Atlantic fishing. The term is said to have originated around the year 1700, coming from a Scottish word for skimming along the water. The name schooner referred to relatively small ships with two masts rigged fore and aft. Their main sails lay along the length of the ship from front to rear. They also carried one or more topsails, and forward or head sails called jibs.

A typical Grand Banks schooner could carry up to eight sails.

Early Nova Scotia schooners, the ancestors of *Bluenose*, were deep, narrow ships which needed a lot of extra weight or ballast to make them sail well. Ballast took up room and cut down on the amount of supplies and fish a ship could carry. Nova Scotian shipbuilders made improvements to the design of their vessels, and by 1910, more efficient schooners were being built. These ships could also sail fast in all kinds of winds.

Although they fished the same waters, schooners built in Massachusetts, where *Bluenose*'s rivals were built, tended to be different from those built in Nova Scotia. They were believed to be faster ships when sailing into the wind, or "windward", than the Nova Scotia schooners.

Fisherman's topsail

Fore gaff-topsail

Jib topsail

Jib

Jumbo

Main gaff-topsail

Mainsail

Foresail

This picture shows the sails on a schooner. Two-masted ships like this one allowed for greater speed.

Starting Early

EDUCATION

Education at that time took place mostly in small one-room schoolhouses. All grades would be taught in the same classroom by one teacher. The high standard of education we enjoy today did not exist. Students were taught basic reading, writing and arithmetic until they left school to work. Other skills emphasized were penmanship (handwriting), enunciation (speaking clearly), and some schools taught agriculture and bookkeeping.

Many children in places like Lunenburg started working early, at an age when today's children are still in school and will be for many more years. Children helped to dry out the catch by putting it on flakes (wooden racks) to be dried by the sun and coastal winds. Angus would likely have done this, as well as helping out with family chores. His father, Elias, insisted that Angus finish schooling before starting the traditional life of a fisherman in one of the simpler jobs. Still, by the age of nine, Angus was begging his father to take him out on his ship, the *Nyanza.*

When he was twelve, Angus spent a summer shovelling salt from the wharf into the schooners which were headed for the banks. The salt was used to preserve the cod catch onboard while the ships were at sea.

In 1895, when Angus was thirteen, Elias finally let him go to sea.

Paying his Dues

WAGES

The amount each crew member earned depended on the size of the ship's catch and the price during that season. Some sailors owned a share of the vessel (known as a "sixty-forth"), which gave them an extra incentive to work harder.

The year before Angus joined the ship, Elias had been the "highliner", which meant that the captain had the ship with the biggest haul of the Lunenburg fleet. Angus was joining a very successful ship.

His first job was as a deckhand. He was a throater. His job was to grab fish that were caught and slit them from throat down to tail.

On Angus's first trip, the cook, who was wearing a derby hat, fell overboard during strong waves at night. Men were sent out in a dory to find him. They saw the hat and went to get it, and were shocked to find that the cook was still underneath! Afterwards, the cook would not be parted from his special life-saving hat.

Angus was given no special treatment; his only breaks were to eat and sleep. It is even likely that Angus, as the youngest crew member, had to do double duty and chase off the sea birds who came to eat the fish.

In Angus's first fishing season, *Nyanza* brought in one hundred tons of fish, again earning her captain the title of highliner of the fleet.

COD LIVER OIL

Oil taken from the livers of cod is rich in vitamins A and D and was once widely used to prevent diseases caused by lack of proper nutrition. It is still sold in some drug stores.

ICEBERGS

An iceberg is a large chunk of ice that has broken off a glacier or ice sheet, like Antarctica. Many are found in the North Atlantic, in the Labrador Current that carries them south toward the banks.

Moving Up

Eventually, Angus was promoted to header. This meant he took the fish from the throater and removed the liver, which was used to make cod liver oil, the head and the guts. After that, the fish were ready to be packed in salt for the homeward journey.

Angus's next job was as a doryman. The crew were up by four in the morning and ready for work. If the sea was calm, dorymen went out in the boats to set the nets, called trawls, and pull them in. On his first trip as a doryman, Angus became lost in a heavy fog. He and his partner in the dory had to spend the night out in the fog, worrying about being lost, before they were found the next day.

Fog was not the only danger; violent storms could come up, and in the north near Labrador, icebergs were also a risk.

Trawling

A dory is a small flat-bottomed boat, made of planks with no keel (the main piece of wood to which the frame of a ship is attached) or rudder (the steering mechanism). It has oars and a rag sail. Dories went out at dawn from the ship with kerosene lanterns. They usually carried bait, a horn, water, mooring, a compass and two anchors. The anchors were attached to the ends of a trawl line (a long line with others branching off it), which could be up to two and a half kilometres long.

There were more than twenty fishing lines in a trawl. Each line carried around eighty hooks. The dorymen would check the lines and rebait them throughout the day, which was slow work that involved checking all the hooks on the trawl lines. Sailors could easily get the barbed hooks caught in their hands. The risk of infection was much more serious in those days, without antibiotics and antiseptics.

COMPASS

A compass is an instrument used to find out where you are on Earth. A compass has a magnetized pointer that aligns itself with Earth's magnetic field, showing north, south, east and west. When used with other navigational instruments, it gave sailors their accurate position on the sea. It is believed that the compass was invented in ancient China.

Supplies

SALTING

Before the age of electric refrigeration, food still had to be preserved, or it would spoil before it reached the consumer. Fish were salted to cure them. Salt kills microorganisms, which are tiny life forms that cause spoilage. The fish could then be stored until the ship reached the shore again.

Before sailing, supplies were brought on board for the long trip out on the banks. It was important that foods be nutritious, easy to prepare and not take up too much valuable room on the ship. Supplies were also needed to keep the catch fresh until it could be brought back to land. On a typical voyage, provisions might be:

—Barrels of fresh drinking water
—Hundreds of pounds of bait
—Tons of salt to preserve fish caught and stored in the hold or in the cook's galley
—Flour
—Potatoes
—Sauerkraut
—Various kinds of dried foods. There were two dried staples:
—"bully-beef" (dried meat which would not spoil when wet)
—"hard-tack" or "ship's-biscuit" (like a big, thick, tough cracker)

Cod drying at a Newfoundland port

LOG

A ship's log is a record of data about weather conditions, activities of the crew and visits to port. It was often filled out daily, since what was reported in it could be important for navigation and weather prediction. A log was not required for fishing vessels, but many captains kept them anyway.

TOOLS

Other navigation tools used were a sextant, a taffrail log, compass and geographical charts. Captains also used "dead reckoning", an educated guess involving such factors as speed and distance travelled, allowing for current and wind, which helped them find their way in the fog.

(see the glossary on page 61 for definitions of nautical terms)

Moving On

Angus spent two years on his father's ship, the *Nyanza*. One spring, the ship struck a patch of ice, ripping a large hole in the hull, and the crew had to escape in the dories. The ship was lost, and Angus went on to work for other captains.

Angus worked on a number of ships. He was learning everything he could, in preparation for the day when he would captain his own ship. There was a lot to learn, about reading the weather, navigation, keeping the ship's log, how to manage a crew, keep their morale up and where to find the best catch of fish. These skills took years to develop.

Angus was in his late teens when he became first mate on a trip to the West Indies. On this trip, his brother John, who was captain, was washed overboard by high waves. Angus took command, and luckily the crew was able to find John before he was swept away into the sea. Angus already knew the dangers of bad weather; he had seen a man lost that way before.

A shipwreck

A Sea Shanty

A is the Anchor that holds a bold ship,
B is the Bowsprit that often does dip.
C is the Capstan round which we must wind, and
D are the Davits on which the jolly boat hangs.

CHORUS:
So hi derry, hey derry, ho derry down,
Give sailors their grog and there's nothing goes wrong,
So merry, so merry, so merry are we,
No mortal on earth like a sailor at sea.

SEA SHANTIES

Sailors sang sea shanties, which were work songs (sometimes called sea chanties) to help them get through the monotonous tasks, to keep morale high and as a social activity. They were sung along with the rhythms of work. Examples of these have been collected from many fishing countries. This example, "The Sailor's Alphabet", which was sung in Atlantic Canada as well as in England and sometimes had slightly different words, is a useful glossary of sailing terms.

Please see page 61 for a glossary of nautical terms such as those used in this song

E is the Ensign, the Red, White and Blue,
F is the Fo'castle that holds the ship's crew.
G is the Gangway where the mate takes his stand, and
H is the Hawser that seldom does strand.
CHORUS

I is the Irons where the stuns'l boom sits.
J is the Jib boom that often does slip.
K are the Keelsons of which you've been told, and
L are the Lanyards that always will hold.
CHORUS

M is the Mainmast so stout and so strong,
N is the Northpoint that never points wrong.
O are the Orders which we must beware, and
P are the Pumps that cause sailors to swear.
CHORUS

Q is the Quadrant the sun for to take,
R is the Rigging that often does shake.
S is the Starboard side of our bold ship, and
T are the Topmasts that often do split.
CHORUS

U's for the uniform, mostly worn aft
V's for the vangs running from the main gap
W's for water, we're on a pint and a pound
And X marks the spot where old Stormy was drowned.
CHORUS

Y's for yardarm, needs a good sailor man
Z is for Zoë, I'm her fancy man
Z's also for zero in the cold winter time
And now we have brought all the letters in rhyme.
CHORUS

His Own Ship

THE OCEAN TRADE

During the off-season, captains made money by going on voyages carrying freight, items like Prince Edward Island potatoes and produce and Newfoundland herring. Some also took cargos of fish to the West Indies, the main market for Nova Scotia salted fish. Sometimes trips were taken even farther afield.

Angus became captain of a ship in 1905 at the age of twenty-four, when many modern young people are still deciding what they want to do for a career.

His first ship was the *Minnie M. Cook,* and his first voyage was to Puerto Rico in the Caribbean Sea with a load of lumber. Angus enjoyed fast sailing ("carrying sail") and practiced on the voyage.

It was not long before he owned his own ship, in 1908. He managed this by the common practice of selling shares to raise money. The shareholders would co-own the ship and take profits from his catches. He named the schooner after his sister, the *Muriel B. Walters.* The ship's first voyage was under charter (meaning it was hired to deliver cargo).

A share in the Bluenose Schooner Company, formed in 1921

A Tough Customer

A LAWSUIT

Angus may have been tough, but he was very sensitive about some things. He once sued an American newspaper that said that he had "cursed the Lord". He got $3500 in damages.

Angus was popular with his men, even though he had the reputation of being very demanding. This was because he never demanded anything of his sailors that he would not do himself. He was regarded as a "first-class fish killer" and a good manager of people.

Angus was not known as a jolly man, rarely smiling, cursing frequently and often showing a stubborn streak. He could be short-tempered when he felt things were not going his way.

But there was no doubt that he was one of the best captains on the banks, and he never had trouble getting crews. Other schooners would follow him because of his reputation for finding the whereabouts of the best catches.

Angus had the reputation of being a "sail dragger", meaning that he pushed the speed of a vessel to the limit and would race with other ships. He had inherited his father's skills as a fisherman and more. William Roué, the designer of *Bluenose*, said of Angus that he was "always a fighter. Nobody put anything over on him in a race."

Angus's grandson Wayne later said: "He never wanted to be better than any other man. Just as good."

Angus Walters at the wheel

Love and War

WORLD WAR I

World War I, also known as the Great War, began in 1914 when the Archduke Franz Ferdinand of Austria was assassinated. Tension between European countries had been building up for some time, and this caused a chain of events that led to a terrible four-year war. The war claimed millions of lives and even dragged North American countries like Canada and the United States into the conflict.

In 1908, at the age of twenty-six, Angus married Maggie Tanner, a nineteen-year-old girl from a fishing family. Like all fishermen's wives, she had to deal with his long absences away at sea. They would have three sons together, Gilbert (1910), Bernard (1911) and Stewart (1915). Until the start of the First World War, Angus fished on the banks.

The First World War (also known as World War I) was a dangerous time for the fishermen. However, they had no choice but to continue to sail. German U-Boats (submarines) could be lurking around at any time and could sink the ships to try and damage Canada's fishing industry. Halfway through the war years, Angus changed ships, selling the *Muriel B. Walters* and buying the *Donald Silver*, which he sailed until the end of the war in 1918.

He then changed ships yet again, to the larger *Gilbert B. Walters*, named after his two sons Gilbert and Bernard. He set a record with this ship for the largest catch of halibut. Angus was developing a reputation as a great captain, and also a fast sailor. The stage was set for his future as the captain of the world's fastest schooner.

A German U-boat from World War I

Racing

AMERICA'S CUP

The America's Cup was the first famous boat racing competition. It was the result of a friendly challenge between England and the United States in 1851, which was won by the U.S. ship, the *America*. The trophy was named after the winner. This high-profile competition still takes place every few years to this day.

GLOUCESTER

Gloucester is one of the oldest ports in the United States, founded by the Pilgrims in the 1620s. By the nineteenth century, it was one of the largest fishing ports in the world.

The International Fishermen's Race Trophy

A friendly rivalry existed among sailors from different territories, and an event like the America's Cup yacht race was one way that they tested their superiority on the seas.

Sometimes English and American ships would race, and sometimes Canadian and American ships would also take each other on.

In 1920, a new race, the First International Fishermen's Race, was held between Lunenburg and Gloucester, Massachusetts. The port of Gloucester was Lunenburg's American equivalent, the fishing centre of the New England states. The race was promoted by the owner of the *Halifax Herald* newspaper, William H. Dennis. A committee raised the four thousand dollar prize money, and there would also be a silver trophy. Only fishing schooners that had worked for a minimum of one season on the banks could compete, and only real fishermen could man the ships. Elimination races would be held in Halifax and Gloucester to determine the two ships that would compete on a thirty-five to forty nautical mile (about sixty-five to seventy-four kilometre) course. The race would have to be completed in nine hours.

23

The First Race

One of William Roué's original blueprint plans for the race course

A SURPRISE

Angus Walters later said that the captains participating in the Canadian elimination races were unaware that there was to be an international race against an American ship. They thought it was just to be between themselves.

Angus Walters entered his ship, the *Gilbert B. Walters,* in the trials for the first race, held in 1920, even though his wife was ill at the time. Unfortunately, he finished second of eight ships in his trial on October 11, when his ship lost a mast. He finished five minutes behind the winner on the forty-mile course. One captain was killed in the race when the boom of his ship knocked him overboard.

The American elimination race was won by a ship called the *Esperanto.*

The Canadian representative, the *Delawana,* faced the *Esperanto* on October 20 and November 1, and the American ship won the trophy in two straight races. The Canadian ship had provided little competition.

The reason why the American ship won may have been because of differences in the construction of the ships. Lunenburg ships were not built for speed, but for carrying capacity. The Gloucester ships carried smaller loads but had to be built for speed in the crowded and competitive east coast American fishing market.

The *Bluenose* is Born

SMITH AND RHULAND

Smith and Rhuland was a successful shipyard in Lunenburg. It was founded in 1900 by Richard Smith and George Rhuland and built almost three hundred vessels. In later years, it built the replicas HMS *Bounty* (1960) and *Bluenose II* (1963). The shipyard closed for good in the summer of 2006 after more than a hundred years of operation.

A group of Halifax businessmen, the Halifax Racing Committee, wanted to give Canada a better chance in the next International Fishermen's Race. In 1921, they asked Angus Walters to captain a special ship that would be designed by Halifax marine architect William J. Roué. Walters agreed to captain the ship as long as he could have a controlling number of shares, meaning that he would be the majority owner of the boat.

Three hundred and fifty shares of one hundred dollars were sold to pay for the building of the ship, and the Bluenose Schooner Company was formed *(see the photo of a share on page 20)*. The new vessel would retain the Nova Scotian carrying abilities but would be able to match the Gloucester ships in speed.

Roué's opinion was that a ship with a low centre of gravity and a minimum of ballast was the answer. Although Roué's first plans were rejected, eventually shipbuilders Smith and Rhuland began to build the ship from his designs.

William Roué

BRIGHT FUTURE

When the design of the *Babette* was shown to a famous American designer, who was told that it was by an amateur, he said, "Well, he won't be amateur for long."

DESIGN

Roué said of his design: "...she is a combination of the Gloucester and Nova Scotia vessels, having the depth of the former and the breadth, freeboard and carrying capacity of the latter."

William J. Roué, who was born in 1879 in Halifax, was a self-taught marine architect, who became one of the world's great ship designers. He had been interested in ships from his childhood. "I was making boats when I was four years old, out of shingles... I had a natural bent for it. Just as some people have a natural bent for music." Roué's only formal training in ship design was a mechanical drawing course—he simply had an inborn talent and an ability to absorb information. He also had a reputation as an excellent sailor.

The first full-sized sailing boat he designed was the *Babette*, a small single-masted vessel launched in 1909. The committee organized to build *Bluenose* knew that a special design was needed to win the International Fishermen's Race, and the young architect was invited to submit a proposal.

After his success with *Bluenose*, Roué went on to design barges used by the Allied forces in World War II. General Dwight Eisenhower, Commander-in-Chief of the European forces, praised them as the finest barges used in the war.

During his distinguished career, two hundred and fifty vessels were built from Roué's designs. He lived past the age of ninety and died in 1970.

The Launch of *Bluenose*

FEATURES

The dimensions of the ship were:
Overall length   43.6 metres
Beam   8.2 metres
Waterline   34.1 metres
Depth main hatch   3.5 metres
Sail area   930 square metres

SHIPWRIGHTS

Being a shipwright was a very skilled trade, and skills were passed down through the generations. They used tools such as the adze, a chisel-like tool used to trim down large timbers into shapes like masts, the drawknife and the spokeshave, used for fine trimming and smoothing. The booms, gaffs and bowsprit were carved by hand by shipwrights.

Despite Angus's skill and his incredible bond with the ship, a good deal of the credit for *Bluenose*'s success must be also given to the design. Angus helped Roué by giving him recommendations. For instance, Angus decided the foc's'le (forecastle, the front compartment) was too low. He had eighteen inches of space added to give the sailors more headroom. William Roué did not agree that this had made the ship faster, although Angus later insisted that it did.

Bluenose, which was constructed at the Smith and Rhuland shipyards, had a long black hull, a curved bow and pointed bowsprit. It was made entirely of Nova Scotian wood, except the masts, which were made of pine from Oregon, in the Western United States. The Governor-General of Canada, the Duke of Devonshire, drove a symbolic golden spike into the timber.

On March 26, 1921, *Bluenose* was launched. A champagne bottle was broken across its bow as it slid into the sea to the crowd's cheers.

A MYSTERY

Richard B. Smith, one of the builders of *Bluenose*, once said: "I can't tell you what was different from *Bluenose* and other ships, and nobody else can. Bill Roué tried to duplicate her lines, but he couldn't. She was a good sailor, a big carrier and a great fisherman."

REFITTING

Refitting a ship for racing after months of fishing on the banks was expensive and time-consuming. All of the fishing gear had to be removed. New sails were made and topmasts added. A complete cleaning had to be done. The ballast had to be changed to make sure that the ship's balance was right for racing.

Working Ship

Before the qualifying races for the next International Fishermen's Race, *Bluenose* spent a season on the banks as a working ship. The ship quickly proved its practical worth by bringing in the largest catch and making Walters the "highliner" of the fleet. Walters also accepted a few racing challenges to test his ship and won them all.

But *Bluenose*'s fame was almost not to be. One night, a sailor on watch spotted a ship in full sail speeding towards them. Despite warnings, the ship did not stop, and Angus ordered the twenty-man crew to prepare to abandon ship in the dories. The other ship missed *Bluenose* by inches, allowing it to go on to meet its destiny.

28

Qualifying

MAYFLOWER

The Americans also had their own elimination races. One special ship was built by an American committee and called the *Mayflower*, after the ship that brought the Pilgrim settlers to America. It was disallowed as an inappropriate fishing ship when the Nova Scotians refused to race against it because it had been built specifically for racing. American efforts to prove otherwise had no effect.

Bluenose had already proved that it was an impressive ship, but in order to compete against America's best, it would have to beat Nova Scotia's best. After the ship had been refitted, on Saturday, October 16, 1921, the first race took place in Halifax.

Five of the seven contestants were Lunenburg schooners. The *Delawana* was back to race for the right to represent Canada on the triangular forty-mile course (sixty-four kilometres). That day, *Bluenose* won the first in the best-of-three race series by a margin of four minutes, then won the second the next day by fifteen minutes.

Bluenose had demonstrated that its talent was sailing hard into the wind. The ship was so good at this that it was called "a witch to windward."

Bluenose was set to represent Canada in the Second International Fishermen's Race.

Bluenose leading in a 1921 elimination race

Bluenose Triumphs

MAYFLOWER AGAIN

Bluenose came across *Mayflower* on its way to the races. The ships had a casual race. *Mayflower* fell behind, but it was not a realistic result because *Mayflower* did not have all of its racing sails up.

JOY

The *Halifax Herald* newspaper described the scene: "As the schooner came up the harbour, the noise of cheering thousands and shrieking whistles was deafening. Everything, ashore and afloat, that had a noise making device attached to it, seemed to add its share to the general pandemonium." The newspaper had numerous proud stories and editorials in its pages the next day.

The American side was represented by a ship called the *Elsie,* captained by Marty Welch. He had also been captain of the *Esperanto,* which had won the previous year's race, but had since sunk. During the first race on October 22, 1921, the *Elsie* lost its fore topmast, but Angus furled his to make sure he did not gain an advantage. He won by a margin of thirteen minutes, setting a course record.

Two days later, on October 24, *Bluenose* finished three miles ahead of the *Elsie.* Angus had won the trophy! There was much celebration in Halifax and Lunenburg over the great honour that *Bluenose* had brought.

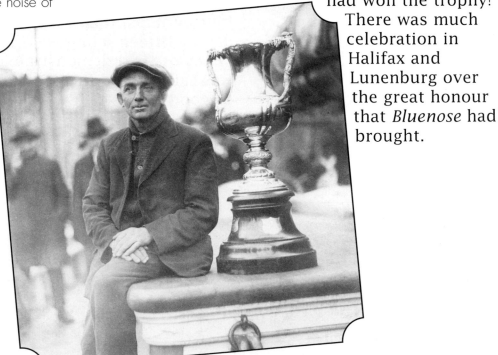

MAHASKA

There was a superstition amongst sailors that it was good luck to have as many a's as possible in a ship's name. This would have made the *Mahaska* a very lucky ship if it were true.

A National Hero

Bluenose's victory had captured the imagination of Canadians. Interest was intense, as "ship to shore" radio had been used for the first time to describe what was happening. People on shore could follow the race as it went on. Parties were thrown around Halifax, and a bottle of champagne was sent to the crew of *Bluenose*, but the sailors preferred their traditional drink, rum.

The International Fishermen's Race was not a one-time event, and *Bluenose*'s title would have to be defended. The ship would again have to compete in a qualification race for the right to represent Nova Scotia.

A competing group of Nova Scotians had built a ship, the *Mahaska,* to contest the race, but it was no match for Angus Walters' ship, and *Bluenose* won again. The captain of the *Mahaska* was said to have jumped up and down on his hat in anger!

They would face the American entry again, the *Henry Ford,* on October 23 to the 26th, 1922, this time in American waters. The *Henry Ford* had won the right to represent the United States, despite being damaged during its launching.

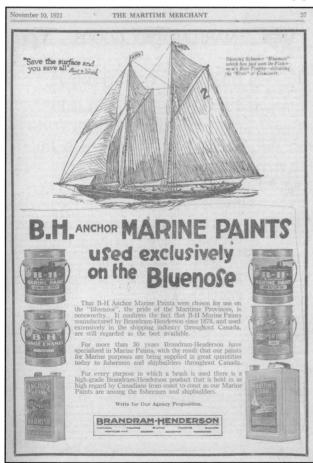

Bluenose's fame was capitalized on by advertisers, as in this 1921 magazine ad

Another Victory

STARLING BURGESS

In many ways Burgess's career paralleled Roué's. He was born in 1870, and his first love was aviation. In 1909, he built a plane that made the first ever flight in New England. He later turned his attention to ships and designed a number of very successful racing ships.

A TELEGRAM

Angus Walters received a congratulatory telegram from the Canadian Prime Minister himself, W. L. Mackenzie King, after the 1922 race.

The Americans had also commissioned their own ship for the 1922 races, designed by a famous marine architect, Starling Burgess. The ship seemed fast but sank off Sable Island in the banks before it could be put to the test.

A second vessel, the *Henry Ford*, was commissioned, and this time the results were closer than in 1921. *Bluenose* lost the first race to the *Henry Ford*, but it was ruled that the American ship had jumped the gun, and the first race was run again. However, the *Henry Ford* won again, putting Walters and his ship against the ropes. They had to win the second race or lose a chance at the title.

Bluenose won the second race, but a heavy wind caused the American ship to lose a mast. The Americans claimed that the result was not fair. Their complaints were not recognized, however, and *Bluenose* won the third race to capture the trophy again. The legend of the unbeatable ship was starting to develop.

Bluenose and the *Henry Ford* in the 1922 final

Canada in the 1920s

Since Canada's confederation in 1867 (the anniversary we celebrate as Canada Day), the country had been growing in independence from its former British rulers. Canada's participation as its own nation in World War I gave Canadians a new sense of pride, which was reflected in the excitement shown after *Bluenose*'s successes on the international stage.

In Nova Scotia, the decade was a difficult one. Halifax had been almost levelled by a terrible explosion in 1917. The province also experienced economic problems, and many industries suffered. Many Nova Scotians felt misunderstood and ignored by the Canadian government. Walters' victories became an important source of pride for Nova Scotians.

HALIFAX, 1917

On December 6, 1917, the *Mont-Blanc*, a ship carrying explosives, blew up in Halifax Harbour after a collision, causing unbelievable devastation. Buildings were levelled for two kilometres around the blast, and thousands of people were killed or injured. It was the largest explosion on record before the invention of the atomic bomb in the 1940s.

Controversy

BUOYS

After the first race in this series, it was decided that the course of the race would be marked out by buoys, floating markers anchored to the ocean floor. The ships would have to pass on the seaward side of these. This rule was introduced for safety after the *Columbia* inadvertently forced *Bluenose* close to shore, causing *Bluenose* to veer back towards the sea and almost collide with the American ship.

Bluenose's American competitors were determined to take the crown away in 1923. They hired the designer of the *Mayflower,* Starling Burgess, to design another schooner to compete with Canada's unbeatable ship. The result was the *Columbia*. It defeated the *Henry Ford* for the right to take on *Bluenose* in the 1923 race. The ship's captain, Ben Pine, would become Angus's greatest adversary in coming years, but also a friend. He had assembled a crew of skilled captains to man his ship.

The 1923 race, held from October 23 to November 1, was also controversial. *Bluenose* won the first race but was almost forced onto rocks by the *Columbia*. *Bluenose* also won the second race in the series but committed a violation by passing a buoy on the landward side. The American side protested, and the race was awarded to the *Columbia*.

Bluenose's fiery captain was furious and refused to race a third time. Walters sailed back to Lunenburg, despite the anger of the International Racing Commitee and against the advice of the ship's managing owner. He felt that he and his crew had been wronged, and he was not afraid to take a stand.

Back to Work

FRIENDS

Angus had a special bond with his ship. He was known to talk to it as if it were alive. Perhaps it was this special bond that allowed him to get the best out of the ship. Angus said about his ship: "There was times where she seemed to be rather lazy about getting under way among some of the other boats, and I would talk to her just the same as I would talk to one of my own. She must have understood, because after a while she made her mind up, why, she'd just say goodbye to the rest of 'em...I think that she was more human than what she was actually, wood and iron."

When *Bluenose* returned to Canada, offers came in from across the country to make up the prize money that Canadians felt the ship was entitled to. The ship and its captain were still heroes, but now it was time to return to work. The International Fishermen's Race would not be held again for eight years. The ship went back to fishing the banks and once again recorded record catches.

In 1925, a group of Halifax businessmen decided to build another ship that could beat *Bluenose*. They went to William Roué, who designed a ship called the *Haligonian*, which was launched at Shelburne, Nova Scotia, in March, 1925. It was similar to *Bluenose*, but it was built lower in the bow. After a season on the banks and a near-grounding, the two ships finally met in 1926. *Bluenose* won a series of three races, although some still argued that the *Haligonian* had what it took to beat Walters' ship. The debate was never resolved.

A Close Call

SABLE ISLAND

Sable Island off the Atlantic coast was known as the "Graveyard of the Atlantic" because so many ships had sunk or been grounded in the waters around it.

DESTRUCTIVE WINDS

The August gales of 1926 and 1927 were two of the biggest storms the fishermen of Nova Scotia had ever seen. In 1927, four Lunenburg schooners were lost, and more than eighty crew members were killed. After these terrible experiences, families started to divide their men on different vessels to reduce the chances of members of the same family being killed in such terrible events.

In April 1926, *Bluenose* was caught up in a storm off Sable Island, a sandy island three hundred kilometres southeast of Halifax. The force of the storm removed the anchor, turning the ship loose. Angus lashed (tied) himself to the wheel to avoid being swept overboard and fought the wind and waves for eight hours. When they arrived home, much of the ship's contents had been lost, but no one had died.

A vicious gale also occurred in August 1926, and again in August 1927, when *Bluenose*'s rival the *Columbia* went down. A year later, a ship's trawling cables pulled up the hull of the *Columbia*, which glided along the water like a ghost ship for a few moments before the cables snapped.

A Defeat

THE STAMP

The fifty cent *Bluenose* stamp was based on a photograph of the 1922 races in Halifax. The stamp is now a rarity seen only in collections.

Gertrude L. Thebaud with a tugboat in the foreground

NO BLAME

Angus later said of the *Thebaud:* "She didn't beat the *Bluenose.* She beat me."

Canada had not forgotten *Bluenose.* A special stamp, the "Fifty-cent Bluenose Commemorative", was issued in January 1929. This blue stamp became prized by collectors. Little did Canadians know that *Bluenose*'s career as a winner was far from over.

The only races the ship was involved in before the 1930s were with the *Haligonian.* In 1929, a group of Bostonians challenged the *Bluenose,* but Walters' ship, which was captained by another man at the time of the incident, ran aground in Newfoundland and was not able to compete.

In 1930, Captain Ben Pine challenged Walters to an unofficial race with a ship called the *Gertrude L. Thebaud.* The race would take place at Gloucester, with a trophy and prize money put up by Sir Thomas Lipton of the Lipton tea company. Two of the races had to be called off because of light winds, but the American ship won two of the three races. New Englanders were ecstatic about the victory, but the International Fishermen's Race trophy was still in Nova Scotian hands.

The American group was now confident enough to issue a challenge for the IFR trophy, which they were sure they could win.

Angus's Greatest Rival

Pine and Walters, rivals and friends

American captain Ben Pine was actually born in Canada, in Belleoram, Newfoundland, and moved to Gloucester, where he worked as a junk dealer. Eventually he started a new business, the Atlantic Supply Company, which outfitted ships with supplies. He was also a fierce competitor and wanted to bring glory to his adopted home in Massachusetts.

He and Angus Walters became friends, but were also very competitive with each other. Angus said: "...we got along all right, except when we started to go to the line... We were friendly, but it made no difference ... we were out to beat him and he was out to beat us." Angus was always ready to give credit to Pine for his good qualities: "...as far as on shore is concerned...Ben Pine had a very big heart. Very good natured. It was nice to be in his company."

1931

A JOKE

Angus sometimes enjoyed a joke at the expense of his rivals. He said in 1931 that "it got very lonely out there without another schooner in sight to keep *Bluenose* company" during a race.

WONDER-VESSEL

The value of *Bluenose*'s victories in raising the profile of Nova Scotia did not go unrecognized. A *Herald* columnist said that "One can scarcely compute the value of such worldwide advertising as this event has afforded us." The newspaper called the ship the "Wonder-Vessel."

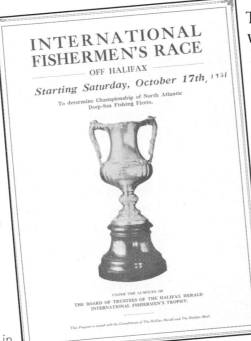

INTERNATIONAL FISHERMEN'S RACE

OFF HALIFAX

Starting Saturday, October 17th, 1931

To determine Championship of North Atlantic Deep-Sea Fishing Fleets.

UNDER THE AUSPICES OF
THE BOARD OF TRUSTEES OF THE HALIFAX HERALD
INTERNATIONAL FISHERMEN'S TROPHY.

This Program is issued with the Compliments of The Halifax Herald and The Halifax Mail

The International Fishermen's Race was scheduled to occur again in 1931. Ben Pine was back with the *Gertrude L. Thebaud*, and he was determined to make this his year.

Three races were run, with one being disallowed because it went over the maximum time. *Bluenose* easily won the other two by thirty-two and twelve minutes. The trophy appeared destined to remain in *Bluenose*'s possession.

Once again, the victory was received with joy in Lunenburg, and a victory parade was held. The *Halifax Herald* declared: "Pride and Joy was in everyone's heart that the *Bluenose,* her captain and crew belonged to Lunenburg...she is even a better sailor than ever." The people of Gloucester declared that the rivalry between *Bluenose* and the *Thebaud* was now tied.

Many felt that this would likely be the last of the races, because diesel engines were taking the place of sails, and the increased use of large trawling nets was threatening to make the doryman's life on a schooner obsolete. Not only that, but fresh fish was becoming more popular and successful than the salted-fish market that ships like the Lunenburg schooners specialized in.

Depression Days

THE GREAT DEPRESSION

In 1929, the stock market in New York crashed in a frenzy of unrest by investors. A decade of good times and spending ended, and a new decade of trying times began. Most industries were badly affected by the Depression.

TOURISTS

Promotional products were sold to fund *Bluenose*'s role as a tourist attraction, including a souvenir booklet and a puzzle.

Bluenose crew in 1933

A PROUD COUNTRY

During *Bluenose*'s visit to Toronto, the *Toronto Telegram* newspaper wrote: "Her name is a household word. She has knit Canada together." In the middle of the Depression, *Bluenose* helped lift the spirits of Canadians.

By this time, the Great Depression was well under way, and the Nova Scotian fishing industry was in decline. Some sailors and captains were driven to bootlegging liquor to earn a living—they could make three hundred dollars per month compared to seventy-five dollars fishing. *Bluenose* remained a fishing ship on the banks, although it was also used for charter cruises along Nova Scotia's South Shore, starting in 1932.

However, the ship's fame did provide Walters with opportunities. In 1933, he was invited to bring *Bluenose* to the Century of Progress Exposition, a World's Fair in Chicago, Illinois, as Canada's representative. A Lunenburg Exhibitor's Company was started to help make it possible. In the summer, the ship sailed down the St. Lawrence, through the Great Lakes to Chicago. Thousands of people visited *Bluenose*, making it one of the most popular and profitable exhibits. The *Gertrude L. Thebaud* was also a popular exhibit at the same fair.

Chicago was a wild town—gangsters shot someone near the ship one night, leading Angus to remark: "She is quite a town. There seemed to be a lot of law but not much justice."

That same summer, *Bluenose* made a stop in Toronto, where it remained for two more seasons and was visited by thousands.

A Great Honour

THE KING AND QUEEN

King George V and Queen Mary were the monarchs of the United Kingdom from 1910 to 1936. During World War I, he changed the royal family's last name from the German Saxe-Coburg-Gotha to Windsor as a patriotic gesture, and it remains Windsor to this day.

ROYALTY

The British monarchy no longer holds political power and is now just a symbol. The queen is still Canada's symbolic head of state, but the governor general, who was once appointed as the monarch's official representative in Canada, is now chosen by the Canadian government.

In 1935, another event helped to cement *Bluenose*'s place in history. This important symbol of a distinct Canadian culture was invited to participate in the Silver Jubilee of King George V and Queen Mary of England. *Bluenose* sailed to Plymouth, England in seventeen days and was received with great enthusiasm. Angus Walters was presented with a sail from the Royal Yacht *Britannia*. Angus had the honour of being presented to the king himself, of whom he said in his down-to-earth way, "He was a very nice, ordinary sort of fella. We chewed the rag a while."

Unfortunately, one day on the journey back to Canada, *Bluenose* was hit by a severe storm. The ship keeled over and was almost overturned, but Walters' and his crew's skills saved the day. The ship had to return to Plymouth for repairs. A British naval commander on board at the time said: "This was the most terrifying sea I have ever encountered. That we are alive today is a tribute to the seamanship of Captain Angus Walters and his crew, and the wonderful qualities of *Bluenose*."

A Changing World

An early
mechanized trawler

The Nova Scotian fishing industry was undergoing some painful changes in the late 1930s. New technology in the form of large mechanized trawler ships was disrupting the lifestyle and livelihood of fishermen who had grown up in the culture.

Fishing had been done the same way, following the same time-tested methods, for generations, but now the modern, mechanized world threatened the way of life of many Nova Scotians. Schooners were no match for ships with engines and trawling nets. Engines would make it possible to fish year round and to sell both to the salt and fresh fish markets. Even *Bluenose* had diesel engines installed in 1936, to try and get profits back up to their old levels.

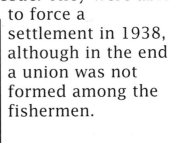

Strike!

FAIRNESS

Angus Walters: "Dealers always argue that it was a poor year. I ask them how they can buy up vessels and draggers at the cost of hundreds of thousands of dollars? I'd like to ask some of them who complain most loudly how much money their fathers left them—money that was made by the sweat of the men who sailed to the banks."

The bad feelings among fishermen led to action in 1937, when a movement began among Nova Scotia's fishermen to get fair wages. They demanded an increase in the price of haddock. Not only did workers support the idea, but many captains as well. Angus Walters was heavily involved in the action and formed alliances with other workers, like the Fishhandlers Union who worked in the plants. At his initiative, the captains tied up the fishing fleet to force the dealers to recognize the issue. They were able to force a settlement in 1938, although in the end a union was not formed among the fishermen.

44

BLUENOSE'S COMPETITORS

Many of *Bluenose*'s competitors met with misfortune over the years:
—*Henry Ford* sank off Newfoundland in 1928.
—*Columbia* sank off Sable Island in 1927.
—*Mayflower* lost her skipper overboard in 1927.
—*Esperanto* sank off Sable Island in 1921.
—*Gertrude L. Thebaud* sank in February 1948 off Venezuela.

FAMILY

Angus and Maggie had three sons. None of them became fishermen—it is said that Angus discouraged them from becoming sailors. Gilbert was a bank manager, Bernard (also "Spike" or BJ) was Town Clerk for the Town of Lunenburg, and Stewart was manager of the Lunenburg Dairy. Bernard donated his father's house for use as a museum in 2000.

A grandson, Wayne Walters, later was the captain of the *Bluenose II*, carrying on the family tradition at sea into the late twentieth century.

What Next?

1937 was the year that *Bluenose* was recognized by being put on the Canadian dime, where its likeness remains to this day *[see page 1 for a photo]*. Also in 1937, Angus's wife Maggie died after a lingering illness.

After all of his achievements and years of hard work on the banks, Angus Walters started to think about his retirement. He was fifty-six years old and ready for a more settled life on shore. In 1938, he met Mildred, the woman who would become his second wife.

He was ready for a change in life, but not before *Bluenose* had its last hurrah in the International Fishermen's Race.

An American group challenged *Bluenose* to race its old adversary in 1938, with a first prize of three thousand dollars.

The wheel cover of the *Bluenose*

One More Time

WORN OUT

Bluenose was worn out after many years on the sea. Before the 1938 race, the ship was repainted and fitted with new sails. The *Halifax Herald* paper said that when considering the condition of the ship, "you will begin to understand just how splendid this latest *Bluenose* win actually proves to be."

TIRED OUT

Angus Walters, who had a strong sense of honour, was upset because he felt all the sportsmanship had gone out of the competition:
"We had proved that the Lunenburg Dutchmen could outsail the American windbags, and then we had to fight for our winnings as well." He also said "the *Bluenose*, as long as I am master, will never race again in the United States." He was correct.

This would be the last of the races for the trophy. The challenger was again the *Gertrude L. Thebaud* and Captain Ben Pine. The government of Nova Scotia helped to outfit the noticeably aging, worn out *Bluenose* for the race, and the Americans put up the prize money. It would be best out of five races in Gloucester, starting on October 9, 1938. This was the only race in the series that was best three out of five. The previous races had been two out of three.

Once again, the races were not without controversy and quarrelling. Captain Ben Pine complained that the races were run in unsuitably heavy weather. The Americans also claimed that *Bluenose* had a lengthened water line, meaning that they thought it was carrying more ballast than the rules allowed. This turned out to be true, so weight had to be taken out. Nonetheless, amazingly at its advanced age and long service, and even though one race was declared void and had to be rerun, *Bluenose* won three of the five races to take the trophy again.

But the controversy was not over. Walters had won eight thousand dollars, but he never received the full amount and had to take legal action to get even five thousand dollars of it. The sour taste left by all this fighting was offset by the fact that Angus Walters and his ship could retire from competition as the unbeatable champions they were.

Preserving *Bluenose*

LOVE FOR A SHIP

Angus's son Spike (Bernard) said that such was Angus's love for the ship that if there was a fire on the ship and a fire in his house, Angus would save *Bluenose* first.

WORLD WAR II

World War II began in 1939 when German dictator Adolf Hitler started claiming other territories in Europe and even invading them. Eventually, almost all European countries were drawn into a war to stop him and his Italian ally Mussolini. Other countries like Japan, Canada, the Soviet Union and the United States had become involved as well. This long war caused unbelievable suffering around the world for six years.

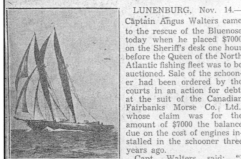

Saves Bluenose
Cap'n Angus Pays $7000 One Hour Before Auction

THE BLUENOSE

LUNENBURG, Nov. 14.— Captain Angus Walters came to the rescue of the Bluenose today when he placed $7000 on the Sheriff's desk one hour before the Queen of the North Atlantic fishing fleet was to be auctioned. Sale of the schooner had been ordered by the courts in an action for debt, at the suit of the Canadian Fairbanks Morse Co. Ltd., whose claim was for the amount of $7000 the balance due on the cost of engines installed in the schooner three years ago.

Capt. Walters said: "I would not see the schooner sold which so faithfully served me, the town of Lunenburg and the owners for over 18 years." The Bluenose is still owned by the Bluenose Schooner Company of which Zwicker and Company are the chief shareholders.

"I have faith in the Bluenose and will have for some time to come and I think it a disgrace the schooner should have been threatened with the auction block. I still will protect the Bluenose with all I have as she served me too faithfully to be let down," Capt. Walters declared.

He said the Bluenose may go fishing in the Spring and added the plan originated by a committee of public spirited men in Lunenburg to take over the Bluenose and preserve her as a memorial had fallen through.

CAPT. ANGUS WALTERS

By 1939, Angus was definitely ready to retire. A movement was starting in Halifax to make the ship a monument and to protect it. There were letter-writing campaigns to newspapers and various fundraisers. One campaign was to form a Bluenose Schooner Company to pay off the $7200 debt for the engines from three years before. The idea was to sell certificates of ownership for a dollar to raise funds. A wealthy citizen opened a bank account to raise money and offered to match any donations, but there were none. Walters had to bid $7200 of his own money to keep the ship that had brought him success and fame.

Angus hired two schooner captains to take the ship to the banks. By this time, the Second World War had begun, and Angus, who was living in Halifax, offered his services to the Royal Canadian Navy. He was now almost sixty and considered too old for active duty, so he returned to Lunenburg. What to do next for a man who loved achievement and hard work?

A New Business

The building that housed the Walters dairy still stands today

Angus and his second wife, Mildred Butler, who was thirty-one years younger than him, were married on Thursday, December 15, 1938 in Halifax, and lived in his house on Tannery Row when they returned to Lunenburg. The house had been built for him in 1915 and has served as a museum in recent years. They started a dairy business in a building next door.

Angus worked hard at his business, and since there had never been a dairy in the town, he prospered. He became involved in local life, becoming a councillor in the town and thus making a further contribution to Lunenburg. He also took up the sport of curling, one of Canada's most popular pastimes in the mid-twentieth century.

Angus found that there was still a great deal of interest in his adventures with *Bluenose*, so he set up a display of his trophies in his dairy office to show visitors.

Angus and Mildred were together until her death at age forty-five in 1957.

CURLING

Curling is one of the most popular sports in Canada. It was likely invented in medieval Scotland. It is played on a rink, and points are won based on the number of "stones" a team is able to slide near a target at one end of the rink. It is a very strategic game that is played all across the country.

The End of *Bluenose*

A TRUE STORY?

Some stories about *Bluenose*'s exploits have never been confirmed. One is that it was stopped by a German submarine, whose captain said: "You are *Bluenose* out of Havana bound for Port Everglades. If I didn't love that boat, I'd shell you right now."

SADNESS

"Schooner Bluenose Lost at Sea", screamed the large headline in the *Herald*. Angus heard about the sinking of his old ship while curling. But he had said farewell to the ship long before, when it was sold.

"If I may say so, there was a lump in my throat. Somehow, I knew it was goodbye. We'd seen a lot together in fair weather and foul, and the *Bluenose* was like a part of me."

In 1942, The West Indies Trading Company made a bid for *Bluenose,* and Angus Walters parted company with his beloved ship, disgusted that no one in Canada had come forward to buy it. *Bluenose* was to become a "tramp schooner".

After selling *Bluenose*, Angus said that on the way home he felt "like I was coming out of the cemetery." *Bluenose* became a sea freighter in the Caribbean, the fishing industry being in a state of collapse. "I felt very bad about it. I thought that she should have been kept here and she should be here today as a memorial to the fishing fleet for what she done and the advertising that she done, not only for this town, but for the whole province of Nova Scotia," Angus said.

On January 28, in 1946, Walters heard the news that the ship had hit a reef off the coast of Haiti and would likely sink. Angus wanted to save the ship and asked for help from the government, but the ship sank the next day—only the engines were saved. One of Canada's greatest icons was gone, but the story of *Bluenose* was not over.

THE OLAND FAMILY

The Oland family opened their first brewery in Nova Scotia in 1867. The family's companies have brewed many popular brands of beer, and they now own the popular Moosehead brand.

Angus Walters drives in the first spike of *Bluenose II*.

HALL OF FAME

Angus Walters was inducted into Canada's Sports Hall of Fame in 1955, another recognition of his great achievements.

Bluenose Reborn

In 1960, Smith and Rhuland, the builder of *Bluenose*, built a replica of the famous eighteenth century British ship, the *Bounty*, for a film adaptation of *Mutiny on the Bounty*. This inspired the building of *Bluenose II*.

In 1963, almost twenty years after the sinking of *Bluenose*, the Olands, a prominent brewing family of Halifax, funded the building of an exact replica of Canada's most famous ship. The ship would be named *Bluenose II*. The plans for the original ship made by William Roué would be used, and the designer himself was consulted on the construction.

On February 27, 1963, the keel was laid, and many of the original workmen who were still alive were back at work on the new ship. Angus Walters helped drive the symbolic golden spike at the start of the building process and was consulted at each stage.

On July 24 of that year, the new ship was proudly launched before a crowd of fifteen thousand people. Angus Walters was on board at the age of eighty-two. He sailed with the ship on its first voyage to the West Indies.

51

An End and a Beginning

Capt. Angus Walters, First Bluenose Skipper Dies

A stirring chapter in Nova Scotia and Canadian history closed last night with the death of Capt. Angus Walters, skipper of the schooner Bluenose, in his home port of Lunenburg.

Born June 9, 1881, Capt. Walters went to sea at the age of 13 when commercial sail design was reaching its zenith for both commerce carrying clipper ships, and for fishing vessels, he reitred after nearly 50 years at sea as chunky, wooden and steel hull trawlers — perhaps much less aesthetically pleasing than the gull-like schooners, but more economical — replaced the sailing vessels as "Queens of the Fishing Grounds."

Born and raised in Lunenburg, he first went to sea as a deck hand on his father's fishing schooner Nyanza, but by the age of 27, in 1908, he had his master's papers and a vessel of his own.

Following the end of the First World War, as a skipper of the Gilbert B. Walters, one of the largest salt-bankers ever to be built in the province, he brought home the largest single catch ever to be landed in the province up to that time — 790,400 pounds straight from the Grand Banks.

But he was most famous for his next schooner, the Bluenose. Built in Lunenburg and launched early in 1921, he outfought, out-smarted, and outsailed his, and Nova Scotia's, bitter sailing and fishing rivals from Gloucester, Mass.,

See CAPTAIN — Page 8

CAPT. ANGUS WALTERS

BIOGRAPHY

A biography of Angus Walters was published in his lifetime, in 1955, titled *Bluenose Skipper* by G.J. Gillespie. This entertaining book is still available in many libraries.

Angus Walters passed away on August 11, 1968, at the age of eighty-seven in Lunenburg and was buried next to the ocean. His name would be forever associated with the great ship he captained to glory, but the story of *Bluenose* still went on in the form of *Bluenose II*. "We're all good fellows when we're dead," he once said, but Angus Walters was already a respected and admired man long before his death.

Bluenose II was given by the Oland family to the province of Nova Scotia as an important contribution to the heritage of the area. The ship would not be a racing or fishing ship, but for passengers only, used to promote *Bluenose*'s legacy and the history of the Nova Scotia fishing trade. It has been a very effective tool for doing just that.

A Different Industry

The fishing industry changed radically after World War II. By the 1950s, "factory fishing" vessels had completely replaced the schooner. They came from all around the world to fish off Canada's coasts. These huge ships use vast trawling nets to catch massive amounts of fish. The technology improved throughout the second half of the century, with record catches peaking in 1968.

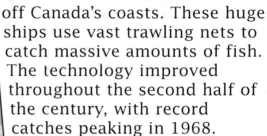

However, companies and governments did not pay enough attention to the issue of conservation, although in 1976 Canada did ban foreign ships from fishing within two hundred nautical miles of the country's shores. But by 1992, an emergency had developed, and the stock of cod was almost depleted. By that year, more than forty thousand people were without work in Newfoundland alone. Within forty years, a once thriving and sustainable industry had been destroyed, relegating the glory days of the Atlantic fishery to history books, story and song. Perhaps one day the northern cod will thrive again off the shores of Atlantic Canada.

Bluenose II's Career

THE MISSION STATEMENT OF *BLUENOSE II*

To continuously promote the history and legacy of *Bluenose* and *Bluenose II* as well as the rich past and present of Lunenburg and Atlantic Canada.

To teach and promote seamanship and life skills in young Canadians through the opportunity of serving onboard *Bluenose II*.

To operate *Bluenose II* in a safe and efficient manner so that all Canadians may be proud.

To maintain and ensure *Bluenose II* will serve as a sailing ambassador for Lunenburg, the Province of Nova Scotia and Canada.

Bluenose II has always spent its summers in Canada's Maritimes, dividing its time between Lunenburg, Halifax and other ports in Nova Scotia. At one time, the ship went south for the winter, carrying charter parties to the Caribbean. The ship also served as host ship at Expo '67 in Montreal.

By 1970, the Oland family had sold their brewery, so they sold the ship to the province of Nova Scotia for one dollar. The provincial government mounted a campaign to raise $250,000 for a refit. Children from across Canada sent dimes with *Bluenose* depicted on them, while the government found corporate donors. It worked, and in 1974, the ship made a goodwill tour to the U.S.

In 1976 it took part in the New York Harbour parade of tall ships, which highlighted the United States bicentennial celebrations. It also travelled to the World's Fair in Vancouver in 1986.

The ship is still active today, offering day trips in its various ports of call.

Lunenburg Today

UNESCO

The United Nations Education, Scientific and Cultural Organization was founded to protect important cultural and historical sites around the world. According to UNESCO, "Lunenburg is the best surviving example of a planned British colonial settlement in North America. Established in 1753, it has retained its original layout and overall appearance, based on a rectangular grid pattern drawn up in the home country. The inhabitants have managed to safeguard the city's identity throughout the centuries by preserving the wooden architecture of the houses, some of which date from the 18th century."

The town of Lunenburg is a very important place in the history of Nova Scotia, and this has been recognized. Though the schooners are long gone, it has been designated a UNESCO World Heritage site, which means that the downtown area by the ocean has been preserved to look as it did in the era when Angus Walters was a young man. The old houses are painted in vibrant colours and the Smith and Rhuland shipyard is preserved. The craft of dory building is still practiced by local craftsmen.

The town is also home to the Fisheries Museum of the Atlantic, which contains displays about the banks fishing industry and the world's largest collection of *Bluenose* artifacts. *Bluenose II* is still based there for part of the summer. The town, which celebrated its 250th anniversary in 2003, is a tourist destination, not only for Canadians and Germans, but for people from all around the world. Nova Scotia's rich history lives on there to this day.

Angus Walters' house in Lunenburg can still be seen today on Tannery Row

Lunenburg today

A Great Legacy

Angus Walters was in many ways the "everyman" of his place and time, a down-to-earth working man who paid little attention to the trappings of success. But he and his ship won an enduring place in the history of Canada and helped to give pride to a new nation discovering its identity.

For eighteen years, *Bluenose* was the undisputed champion of North Atlantic racing. No challenger, no matter how fast or well-skippered, could beat it. In 1988, the government of Canada issued another stamp honouring the legacy of *Bluenose*, with Angus Walters' face on it. It symbolized the spirit of the hard-working people of the country as well as the great fame that Angus Walters had earned. The story of the loving bond between man and ship and their great achievements is one that Canadians will never forget. *Bluenose* was truly, in the words of a poet, "The Sovereign of the Seas."

RENOWNED IN SONG

Bluenose has been remembered in many books, television programs and songs. One song is by the late famous folksinger Stan Rogers. It is called "Bluenose" and is on his album *Turnaround*.

Angus Walters' life and times

1881	June 9, James Angus Walters is born in Lunenburg, Nova Scotia.
1895	Angus goes to sea for the first time on his father's ship, the *Nyanza*.
1905	Angus becomes captain of his first ship, the *Minnie M. Cook*.
1908	Angus buys his first ship, the *Muriel B. Walters*. He marries his first wife, Maggie Tanner.
1910	Angus's first son, Gilbert, is born.
1911	Angus's second son, Bernard, is born.
1915	Angus's third son, Stewart, is born.
1918	Angus buys his third ship, the *Gilbert B. Walters*.
1920	The first International Fishermen's Race is held—the *Esperanto* defeats the *Delawana*.
1921	March 26, *Bluenose* is launched. October, *Bluenose* defeats the *Elsie* to win the trophy for the second International Fishermen's Race.
1922	October, *Bluenose* defeats the *Henry Ford* to win the trophy for the third International Fishermen's Race.
1923	October/November, the fourth International Fishermen's Race is held—no winner is declared.
1926	*Bluenose* defeats the *Haligonian* in a series of three races. April, *Bluenose* is caught in a storm off Sable Island.
1929	January, the "Fifty-cent Bluenose Commemorative" stamp is issued.
1930	October, *Bluenose* is defeated by the *Gertrude L. Thebaud* in the Lipton Cup Race.
1931	October, *Bluenose* defeats the *Gertrude L. Thebaud* to win the trophy for the fifth International Fishermen's Race.
1933	*Bluenose* represents Canada at the Century of Progress Exposition in Chicago, Illinois.
1933-34	*Bluenose* spends two seasons in Toronto, Ontario.
1935	*Bluenose* participates in the Silver Jubilee of King George V and Queen Mary in Plymouth, England.
1936	*Bluenose* has diesel engines installed.
1937	January, *Bluenose* first appears on the Canadian dime.

	Angus is involved in a strike among the Nova Scotia fishermen. Angus's first wife, Maggie, dies.
1938	The Nova Scotia fishermen's strike is settled. October, Bluenose defeats the *Gertrude L. Thebaud* to win the sixth and last International Fishermen's Race. December 15, Angus marries his second wife, Mildred Butler.
1939	Angus pays $7200 to buy *Bluenose*.
1942	Angus sells *Bluenose* to the West Indies Trading Company.
1946	January 29, *Bluenose* sinks off the coast of Haiti.
1957	Angus's second wife, Mildred, dies.
1963	July 24, *Bluenose II* is launched.
1968	August 11, Angus dies at the age of eighty-seven.

About the Authors

Teri-Lynn Janveau was born in North Bay, Ontario. She attended the University of Toronto and Seneca College. She has worked as a library technician for Centennial College, the University of Toronto and the Canadian National Institute for the Blind. She also does freelance research work.

Allister Thompson was born in the United Kingdom and moved to Canada at a young age. He also attended the University of Toronto and has worked in the book publishing industry as an editor for ten years. He is also a folk musician and has recorded several albums. The authors live in Toronto, Ontario.

A holiday in Nova Scotia in 2003 and a shared interest in folklore and history inspired the authors to write the first illustrated children's biography of Angus Walters and his famous ship.

Acknowledgements

The authors would like to thank the following for their assistance in the preparation of this book: Ralph Getson, Curator of Education at the Fisheries Museum of the Atlantic for answering many, many questions with good humour, Sueann Bailey at the FMA and Gary Shutlak and Angelee Vohra at the Nova Scotia Archives for photo acquisition assistance, Chris Berg for last minute assistance, and Sylvia McConnell of Napoleon for entrusting us with this project. We would also like to thank Samantha Thompson for her artistry and our families for their interest and support.

Glossary

Adze: an axe-like cutting tool that has a thin, curved blade set at right angles to the handle and is used chiefly for shaping wood.

Anchor: a heavy iron hook or instrument, usually connected to a vessel by a chain or rope, that is used to grip the bottom of the sea to keep the ship from drifting.

Ballast: heavy material, such as iron, lead, stones or gravel placed in the bottom of the hold to keep the vessel steady in the water.

Banks: an underwater plateau, part of the continental shelf, that rises up from the ocean floor, creating shallow water where fish feed.

Beam: the widest part of a vessel.

Boom: a horizontal spar attached to the bottom edge of a sail used to extend the foot of the sail.

Bow: the forward end of a vessel.

Bowsprit: a long spar attached to the jib boom in the bow used to carry the stays that secure the head sails for the fore-topmast.

Bully-beef: dried or cured meat that does not spoil when wet.

Buoy: a distinctively marked object that floats in the water as a navigational aid.

Capstan: a vertical, spool-shaped cylinder that is rotated manually or by machine to hoist weights such as an anchor or for raising heavy sails.

Carrying sail: sailing fast.

Davits: small cranes that project over the side of a ship used to raise and lower equipment, cargo, or smaller boats to or from the deck of the vessel.

Dory: a small, flat-bottomed rowing boat manned by one or two fishermen and used for fishing from a larger vessel in the open ocean.

Dragger: a fishing boat equipped to tow gear, such as a trawl net, along the bottom of the ocean.

Drawknife: a woodworker's knife to shave surfaces.

Ensign: a national flag or banner carried by a ship.

Fishery: the industry or practice of catching, processing, or selling of fish, shellfish or other aquatic animals.

Flakes: wooden platforms used for drying fish.

Flunkey: an all-purpose labourer on a vessel.

Fo'castle (forecastle): the extreme forward compartment or the living space of the crew in a sailing vessel.

Freeboard: the minimum vertical distance from the surface of the water to the upper deck level, measured at the centre of the ship.

Gaff: a free-swinging spar attached to the top of a four-sided sail.

Galley: the kitchen area for food preparation on a ship.

Gangway: a passage along either side of a ship's upper deck or the ramp used to embark or disembark a vessel.

Grog: an alcoholic beverage, usually rum diluted with water.

Hard-tack: a very hard, unsalted biscuit or bread, also called ship biscuit.

Hatch: an opening in the deck of a ship for entering below or a compartment on a ship.

Hawser: a large, heavy rope made of three strands for nautical use.

Header: removes the heads and entrails from the fish.

Highliner: the captain of the ship with the biggest catch of the season for the fleet.

Hold: a large compartment below the deck of the ship for stowing cargo and supplies.

Hull: the main body of a ship, excluding the deck, masts, rigging and cabin

Jib: a triangular foresail set in front of the foremast.

Keel: the most important timber at the very bottom of the hull to which the stem, sternpost, and the ribs are attached.

Keelsons: a timber or beam that is attached above and parallel to the keel of a ship for added strength.

Landward: in the direction of land.

Lanyard: a short rope or line used for fastening something or securing rigging.

Mainmast: the principal mast of a sailing ship that has two or more masts.

Mast: a large, wooden, vertical spar or pole used to hold up the sails.

Mooring: equipment, such as anchors or chains, for securing a vessel.

Nautical mile: a unit of length used in sea navigation that equals about 6,076 feet (1,852 metres).

Quadrant: an instrument used for taking angular measurements.

Rigging: the lines, ropes, or chains that support the masts and are used for hoisting, lowering or trimming the sails.

Rudder: a fin or blade attached under the hull's stern that moves laterally and is used for steering.

Sail dragger: someone who pushes the speed of a vessel to the limit and races with other ships.

Schooner: a sailing ship rigged with fore and aft sails on two or more masts.

Sea shanty: a rhythmic shipboard working song sung by sailors.

Seaward: in the direction of the sea.

Sextant: a navigational instrument containing a graduated 60° arc, used for measuring angular distances between objects, such as the altitudes of celestial bodies to determine latitude and longitude.

Shipwright: a carpenter who builds and repairs ships.

Shipyard: a yard or enclosure where ships are built or repaired.

Sounding lead: the metal weight or bob at the end of a sounding line.

Sounding line: a line with marked intervals and weighted at one end used to measure the depth of the water.

Spike: a long, thick, sharp-pointed implement made of wood or metal.

Splitter: A person who removes the backbone of the fish and splits it open for salting.

Spokeshave: a kind of drawing knife or planing tool originally for shaping spokes, now used for making rounded edges.

Starboard: the right hand side of a ship when facing forward.

Stuns'l (studding sail): a light sail set at the side of a principal or square sail of a ship in free winds to increase speed.

Taffrail log: a torpedo-shaped log with rotary fins drawn through the water to measure the vessel's speed and distance sailed.

Throater: A person who cuts the throats of the fish open when they are brought on board.

Topmast: a second spar carried above the fore or main mast used to fly more sail.

Topsail: a sail set above the gaff on a schooner, often the second sail in ascending order from the deck.

Tramp schooner: a schooner that carries goods from one place to another.

Trawl: a long, buoyed fishing line holding many shorter lines with baited hooks.

Trawler: a fishing vessel used for trawling.

Trawling: a method of catching fish by pulling a large fishing net through the water behind one or more boats.

Vang: a rope running downward from the peak of the gaff to the ship's rail or mast, used to keep the gaff steady.

Waterline: the line on the hull made by the surface of the water when a ship has the full proportion of stores and crew on board.

Wharf: a landing place or platform built out from the shore into the water where ships may pull up to load or unload cargo, passengers, etc.

Windward: the direction from which the wind is blowing.

Yard: a long, horizontal spar that is tapered at the end used to support a square sail.

Yardarm: part of the yard lying between the lift and the outer end.

Resources that were used in writing this book

BOOKS:
Bluenose by Brian and Phil Backman (Toronto: McClelland and Stewart, 1965)

Bluenose and Bluenose II by Keith R. McLaren (Toronto: Hounslow Press, 1981)

Bluenose, Queen of the Grand Banks by Feenie Ziner (Philadelphia: Chilton Book Co., 1970)

Bluenose Skipper: the Story of Bluenose and Her Skipper by G. J. Gillespie (Second edition, Fredericton: Brunswick Press, 1964)

Captain Angus Walters by Jacqueline Langille (Famous Maritimers series, Tantallon, N.S.: Four East Publications, 1990)

Historic Lunenburg: the Days of Sail, 1880-1930 by Mike Parker (Images of Our Past series, Halifax: Nimbus Publishing, 1999)

Nova Scotia: Shaped by the Sea: a Living History by Lesley Choyce (Toronto: Penguin Books, 1997)

The Promise of Schooling: Education in Canada, 1800-1914 by Paul Axelrod (Themes in Canadian Social History series, Toronto: University of Toronto Press, 1997)

The Saga of the Bluenose by Ernest Fraser Robinson (St. Catharines, Ont.: Vanwell Publishing, 1998)

A Spirit Deep Within: Naval Architect W. J. Roué and the Bluenose Story by Joan E. Roué (New edition, St. Catharines: Vanwell Publishing, 2002)

PERIODICALS:
"The Bluenose" by Silver Donald Cameron (*Canadian Geographic,* vol. 104, April May 1984)

The Halifax Herald (various issues, 1921-1946)

VIDEOS:
The Captain & the Queen (The Canadians series, Great North Productions, 1998)

The Queen and the Skipper: the Story of Bluenose (The Canadian Experience series, CBC, 2004)

WEBSITES:
Bluenose: A Canadian Icon
A virtual exhibit from the Nova Scotia Archives and Records Management featuring more than 350 images relating to Angus Walters, *Bluenose* and *Bluenose II*
http://www.gov.ns.ca/nsarm/virtual/bluenose

Bluenose II
The website of the official operator of Bluenose II
http://museum.gov.ns.ca/bluenose

Explore Lunenburg.ca
The official website of the town of Lunenburg
http://www.town.lunenburg.ns.ca

Fisheries Museum of the Atlantic: A Part of the Nova Scotia Museum
The official website of the museum, which houses the world's largest collection of Bluenose artifacts
http://museum.gov.ns.ca/fma

William J. Roué
A website dedicated to Canada's first naval architect featuring details of his life and career
http://www.wjroue.com/index.html

Index

Photo and Art Credits